the

marriage

preparation

course

**Leaders'
and Support
Couples'
Guide**

© Alpha International 2010

First published 2003

Reprinted 2005, 2007

This edition 2010
Revised 2013
Reprinted 2014

ISBN: 978 1 909309 04 3

Published by Alpha International, Holy Trinity Brompton, Brompton Road, London SW7 1JA.

Email: publications@alpha.org

Contents

Appendices

Introduction

We have been running The Marriage Preparation Course at Holy Trinity Brompton (HTB) since 1985. During that time, the course has changed and developed. We started with a few couples in our home and now hold the course three times a year with more than 100 engaged couples on each course.

The best time to start supporting couples is right at the beginning, before they marry. In today's climate, with so much marital breakdown, more people are aware of the need to prepare. The choice to marry, no longer an assumption in our society, presents a key moment for learning. Our experience has shown us that many couples are open to receiving help as they approach this lifelong commitment and that they enjoy the experience of learning more about marriage and about their fiancé(e). This is what two couples, who completed the course, said a year or so into their marriage:

'The Marriage Preparation Course was invaluable to us as a couple. Although we had been going out together for four and a half years and thought we knew everything there was to know about each other, we learnt so much and have benefited from it immensely. The testimonies from other married couples have really stuck with us and help even today. On top of that we thoroughly enjoyed each evening.'

'We found that many issues we'd never thought about discussing came up when we did Marriage Prep. Our relationship has deepened and our expectations of marriage and of each other are even greater and more exciting than they were before. We thoroughly enjoyed the course and gained so much practical advice from it, which I believe we will use for years to come!'

The course is now available for others to use, whether in a large group, or with one or two couples at home. Some groups prefer to use the DVDs to run the course, while others like to give the talks themselves. Whichever you prefer, this manual will help you. We also recommend that before you run your first course, you watch The Marriage Preparation Course training for leaders found in the Leaders' section of the Relationship Central website.

We now run the course in conjunction with The Marriage Preparation Course Couple Survey and support couples (married couples who go through the results of the survey with each engaged couple). We have found this to be an excellent combination to prepare couples for marriage (see Section D for more details), but the course can be run without these elements and no mention is made of the Couple Survey on the DVDs.

We hope that you enjoy using The Marriage Preparation Course and that it is a blessing to you and to the couples who attend.

Nicky and Sila Lee

A. What is involved?

1) The aim of the course

The aim of The Marriage Preparation Course is to provide engaged couples with the tools to build a healthy marriage that will last a lifetime.

Over five evenings spent together they will:

- learn how to make a marriage work
- consider the importance of commitment
- have the opportunity to recognise their differences
- learn the skills necessary for their relationship to develop and grow
- discuss how to nurture their friendship
- learn about listening and expressing feelings, spending time together and resolving conflict
- understand how to make each other feel loved
- discuss how to develop their sexual relationship
- recognise the importance of talking about their goals, values and dreams

Their privacy as an engaged couple is always respected. There is no requirement to disclose anything personal to a third party. But they are given plenty of opportunities to talk to their fiancé(e) during the discussion times.

2) The guests

The Marriage Preparation Course is for any engaged couple who wants to give their marriage the best possible start. The length of their engagement does not matter and they may or may not have fixed a wedding date. While the course emphasises and explains the unique nature of marriage, we welcome couples who are living together and who want to explore marriage.

Although the course is based on Christian principles, it is suitable for those with no Christian faith or church background and couples do not need to be getting married in a church to come on the course. Over half the people who do the course at HTB are not regular churchgoers and, from the feedback we have received, they find the course very helpful. They are not required to do or say anything that would conflict with their own beliefs. But they are given the opportunity to reflect on their core values and to consider how a shared faith strengthens a marriage. For some people it has provided the first contact with the church and a number of couples have gone on to do Alpha.[1]

Many guests are Christians who are planning a church wedding, and the course enables them to reflect on the part their faith will play in their marriage as well as to acquire the practical tools needed to build their relationship.

3) The design of the course

The course takes place over five evenings and is best run over five weeks (although the material can be fitted in over a weekend or two Saturdays). The evening sessions start at 7 pm with a meal and finish by 9.45 pm at the latest.

Each session consists of a meal followed by short talks interspersed with exercises and questions for each couple to discuss. The course is designed to allow the couple as much time as possible to talk through the issues raised during the session. Each evening a married couple is interviewed and asked what they have learned about marriage, particularly regarding the topics for that session.

4) The set-up of the room (see Appendix 1)

The environment is crucial to the success of the course. Attention to detail is important and greatly appreciated by the couples. The room is set up before the guests arrive. The atmosphere needs to be warm and welcoming so that the couples feel that we value them and their relationship.

---

1 Alpha is a fifteen-session practical introduction to the Christian faith designed primarily for non-churchgoers and new Christians

The lighting is kept low and music is played both during the meal and while the couples are doing the exercises and talking with their fiancé(e).

The room is arranged with tables, tablecloths, table napkins and candles, with three or four engaged couples around each table. There needs to be sufficient space for each couple's conversations to remain private. Background music during the discussion times also helps to ensure privacy.

The set-up may be different for smaller courses being run in a home.

5) The structure of an evening

The evening, including the meal, lasts for up to two hours and forty-five minutes.

Welcome

Guests are welcomed warmly by the leaders. A drink is served and the couples are introduced informally to one another. If the course has more than five or six couples, name badges are helpful.

The meal (30 minutes)

This contributes to the effect of the whole evening. Guests sit with at least two other engaged couples. This is the opportunity for engaged couples to meet each other. We work out in advance who goes with whom according to where they live and their ages and experience of life.

There is a main course only because coffee, tea and dessert are served later in the evening during one of the discussions. Many couples have commented that the meal has made the evening special for them and has given them a chance to relax together after work.

Notices and review (5 minutes)

After the welcome and notices (if any), the couples are given the opportunity to review the topics covered in the previous session(s).

Talks and discussion

Throughout this guide, instructions in white boxes relate to courses on which the talks are given by live speakers. Blue shading relates to courses on which the course DVDs are used.

Live talks: short talks are interspersed with exercises and times of discussion for each couple to do on their own. The couples stay at their tables for the talks and their discussions, although they do not discuss anything with another couple. The talks may also be illustrated with DVD reports, street interviews and short one to two minute interviews which are available online, entitled *The Marriage Preparation Course Inserts*, in the Leaders' section of the Relationship Central website.

DVDs: the DVDs include instructions of when and for how long to stop the tape to give couples the opportunity to do the exercises. The length of the exercises varies between five and fifteen minutes.

Interview

Live talks: each evening a married couple is interviewed for around five minutes about what has been important in their own relationship, particularly with regard to the topics covered on that session. The recorded interview on the DVD could be used instead.

DVDs: a five-minute interview is provided for each week, as well as the shorter interviews with the 'sofa couples' on the topics under discussion.

Concluding remarks and prayer

Live talks: each session finishes with a reading of one of the passages from the Bible suggested as a possibility for their wedding service (see Appendix 4 of *The Marriage Preparation Course Guest Manual*) followed by a short prayer. The recorded readings on the DVD could be used instead.

DVDs: the reading and prayer are provided for you, if you wish to use them.

B. Setting up
a course

1) Course leaders

The course is best led by a Christian couple who has the desire to help engaged couples build a marriage that will last a lifetime. They should have the support of their church leader. They will need to have some experience of leading groups and a willingness to share openly from their own marriage if they are giving the talks themselves.

There should be no major unresolved issues between them when they start to lead the course and they must both be committed to continuing to build their own marriage. For this reason, we recommend that leaders should first do The Marriage Course (a seven-session course designed for married couples to strengthen their relationship) before leading The Marriage Preparation Course.

2) Professional help

The leaders need to have identified a counsellor in their locality to whom they would be happy to refer couples or individuals should issues arise that are beyond their own experience and training.

For large courses, a list of counsellors should be available, specifying each counsellor's area of expertise, whether or not they are Christians, how much (if anything) they charge and how to make contact with them.

3) Volunteer team

The volunteer team supports all aspects of the course including:
- Setting up the room
- Preparing the meal
- Serving the meal
- Clearing and washing up
- Helping to serve tea and coffee
- Music and audio visual support

The number of helpers required will depend on the size of the course. Even with a course of two or three couples, the leaders will benefit from having others who can help them with the logistics of the food and drink so that they are free to give their full attention to the guests.

On the second and subsequent courses, guests from the previous course are invited to help with the practical aspects of the next course. Many couples are glad of the opportunity to give something back as well as to hear some of the talks again.

4) Resources required
(See Appendix 8)

- *The Marriage Preparation Course Leaders' Training* (for leaders and their team to watch before running the course, available in the Leaders' section of the Relationship Central website)
- A copy of this guide for each leader
- A manual for each of the guests (ie two per couple)
- The course DVD set (either to help the leaders with preparation for live talks or to play to the engaged couples)
- Spare set(s) of the DVDs for couples who miss an evening
- *The Marriage Book* by Nicky and Sila Lee (Alpha International, 2010). Each couple receives a copy of the book on the first evening. The cost maybe included in the cost of the course
- Music (suitable music is suggested in on the Relationship Central website). We recommend making a playlist for each session
- Tables and chairs
- Tablecloths, candles, candleholders and table napkins
- Cooking, coffee and tea making facilities
- Equipment for playing the DVDs
- Lectern or other stand for speakers' notes

5) Preparation for each session

The course can be done with the DVDs or by giving the talks live (or by using a combination of these methods). The DVDs clearly indicate when and for how long to pause for each exercise. If doing their own talks, the leaders will need to look at the timetable for each evening to know when to stop for the exercises and discussions (see Section C).

Live talks

If you are giving the talks yourself, start your preparation at least one week beforehand. The speakers' notes are available in the Leaders' section of the Relationship Central website under *The Marriage Preparation Course Toolkit*. These notes also contain the timelines for each session. The speakers' notes may be adapted to include illustrations from your own marriage and may be shortened.

It is important that husband and wife share the speaking in order to give both a male and female perspective and also to reinforce the biblical view of complementarity. You may find that one of you feels more drawn to the theory and the other to the practical outworking of it. Allocate the speaking according to gifts and personality.

The following will be helpful in preparing to lead the evening together if you are giving your own talks as a couple:

- Start your preparation with a prayer
- Watch the DVD of that session and read the relevant section of *The Marriage Book* (see Section C for which section of the book relates to each session of the course)
- Talk through the issues raised in the session and any concerns you have
- Decide who will do each section of the talks
- Work out what you are going to use from your own experience. Go through this with each other to make sure that you are agreed about what you will say. Do not include anything that would offend, belittle or upset your husband or wife
- Adjust the speakers' notes adding your own illustrations
- Make sure you feel comfortable with the material and are familiar with the exercises
- Prepare the couple giving the testimony. Ideally, they should be in their first few years of marriage so that the engaged couples can relate more easily to their experience.

The main aim of the testimony is to illustrate the points made in the talks from their own experience. The testimony should last about five minutes. Choose couples who are willing to be honest and specific and who can add humour to the evening. Both the husband and wife should be interviewed and asked questions that will keep the testimony personal and relevant to the engaged couples. Alternatively, leaders may choose to use the testimonies from the *Inserts* available online

6) Couples who miss a session

We loan the DVD set to couples who are unable to attend one or more of the sessions, in return for a deposit of the replacement value. This allows couples, if they wish, to keep the DVDs so that they can refer to them again in the future.

7) Feedback

A questionnaire has been developed to be distributed on the last evening (see Appendix 2). This serves as a review of the course for the guests and provides helpful feedback for the leaders to know how to make the course more effective the next time. You can print this from the Leaders' section of the Relationship Central website.

The questionnaire can also provide useful quotes to promote the course. These comments should be kept anonymous unless the engaged couple gives permission for their names to be used.

8) Promotion of the course

The message

Whatever the setting, the message to the engaged couples is the same: 'Make the best start to your marriage by preparing for it.' We make it clear that any couple is welcome whether or not they are members of a church. We also assure them that during the course they will not be required to talk about their relationship to anybody else, but that there will be plenty of opportunities to discuss important issues with each other.

Invitations to the course, with the information given above, the dates of the next course and an outline of the topics covered, should be made as widely available as possible. (See Appendix 3 for a sample invitation. These can be personalised for your course at alphaprintshop.org). They could be displayed in church, at register offices, in health centres and at events likely to attract engaged couples. The more invitations in circulation the better.

Most couples come on the course at HTB through the recommendation of another couple who has previously completed the course. Once couples from outside the church start to attend and enjoy it, they spread the message to their friends.

Working with other churches

You may want to work together with other local churches to provide preparation for couples planning to get married in church. You will need to gain the support of the other churches and together create a plan for the publicity and running of the course. This approach encourages local co-operation and sharing of resources. One larger course may initially attract more attention than several small ones and draw in couples not planning to marry in a church.

Community Marriage Policies

A number of places in the UK have started to run 'Community Marriage Policies'. These policies bring together clergy, teachers, doctors, health visitors and others working in the community to encourage people to invest in their relationships through attending marriage and marriage preparation courses.

Some Community Marriage Policies have led to an agreement among the clergy in the area that they will expect all the couples they are marrying to attend a marriage preparation course.

Registering a course

If you are planning to run The Marriage Preparation Course, please let us know via our website at relationshipcentral.org. If you have any queries, please email us at relationshipcentral@alpha.org. This will enable us to support you in the future and direct any enquiring engaged couples in your area to your course. We can also advertise your course on the website if you would like us to, so that any engaged couple wanting to attend can find one within reach of where they live.

Session 1 – Communication

1. Overview

Effective communication is essential for a strong marriage. This session considers how communication is affected by personality, family background and circumstances. Couples look at what it means to talk about their feelings and they practise listening to each other.

2. Resources

- *The Marriage Book* – Section 2

- *The Marriage Preparation Course* script for Session 1 (available *online for live talks*)

- *The Marriage Preparation Course Inserts* (available online for live talks)

- *The Marriage Preparation Course* DVD, Session 1

3. Checklist

- Manual for each guest
- Music during:
  - the meal
  - the exercises and discussions
- Name labels (if the number of couples warrants them)
- Cold drink on arrival
- The meal

- Tea, coffee and dessert
- Tables, tablecloths and chairs
- Table napkins, candles and candleholders
- Spare pens
- Table with recommended books (see Appendix 4)

- Speakers' lectern (for large courses)

- Guest attendance list

- For live talks, an issue to use in the leaders' demonstration of effective listening (this is needed for Session 1 only)

4. Timetable

The timing for the length of each talk is approximate – time allowed for the exercises should not be shortened.

From 6.30 pm – Be ready!

Guests often arrive early on the first evening
Welcome and offer a drink

7 pm – Meal

Main course only

7.30 pm – Notices

- *'Please write your name on your manual'*
- *'Let us know if you can't come for one of the evenings and we will loan you the DVD in return for a deposit'*
- *'Relax! There is no group work. Many people have two fears about coming on a course like this. One is that they will be required to talk to others about their relationship. The other is that their fiancé(e) might talk to strangers about their relationship!'*
- *'We put you in a group over the meal to give you the opportunity to meet one or two other engaged couples'*

Icebreaker

This part is entirely optional and is designed to help everyone get to know another couple better. Ask the couples to tell another couple they are sitting with:

- when they are getting married (if they are already engaged)
- where they first met (there may be two versions for this!)

DVD: Play the DVD. Session 1 lasts for 48 minutes, but in addition you will need to allow 40 minutes for the exercises:

- How we communicate (at 17'13") – allow 5 minutes
- Family styles of communication (at 20'58") – allow 10 minutes (during which drinks and dessert are served)
- Effective talking (at 33'47") – allow 10 minutes
- Effective listening (at 46'03") – allow 15 minutes

This means the whole session takes **1 hour 28 minutes.**

Live talks

7.40 pm	**Talk** – *The value of marriage preparation*
8 pm	**Discussion** (if using the Couple Survey) *'Spend a few minutes asking your support couple any questions you may have about the Couple Survey'*
8.05 pm	**Talk** – *Learning to communicate*
8.15 pm	**Exercise** – How we communicate
8.20 pm	**Talk** – *Learning to communicate (cont)*
8.25 pm	**Exercise** – Family styles of communication (during which coffee, tea and dessert are served to the engaged couples by the leaders and support couples)
8.35 pm	**Talk** – *Learning to communicate (cont)*

8.45 pm   **Testimony** – By a married couple who talks about their own experience of learning to communicate effectively in their marriage (or show testimony on DVD)

8.50 pm   **Exercise** – Effective talking

9 pm   **Talk** – *Learning to communicate (cont)*

9.10 pm   **Leaders' demonstration of effective listening** – Before the evening, one of you needs to have thought of an issue that is bothering you that you have not previously discussed. Do not choose an issue that would be hurtful or embarrassing to your husband or wife. Model the steps for effective listening in the exercise in the guest manual

9.15 pm   **Exercise** – Effective listening

9.30 pm   **Conclusion**

- *'The homework is not the sort we take in and mark! It is designed to help you to follow up the topic of that (or the next) session on your own'*

- *'We will finish each evening by reading one of the passages suggested as a possibility for your marriage service in Appendix 4 of* The Marriage Preparation Course Guest Manual*'*

- Read Colossians 3:12–17 (or show reading on the *Inserts* available online)

- Close the session with a short prayer, eg: *'Lord, thank you that you are the God of love. Thank you that you always listen to us. Please help us to put on love and to be good at listening to each other. Amen'*

Session 2 – Commitment

1. Overview

Commitment lies at the heart of the marriage covenant and is reflected in the marriage service vows. Couples consider the meaning of these vows and then look at how to live out this commitment through making quality time for each other on a regular basis and separating appropriately from their parents.

2. Resources

- *The Marriage Book* – Sections 1 and 6 and Epilogue (Chapter 20)
- *The Marriage Preparation Course* script for Session 2 (available online for live talks)
- *The Marriage Preparation Course Inserts* (available online for live talks)
- *The Marriage Preparation Course* DVD, Session 2

3. Checklist

- As for Session 1
- Spare guest manuals

- For live talks: two separate sheets of differently coloured paper and two sheets stuck together with glue

4. Timetable

From 6.45 pm
Welcome guests with a drink

7 pm – Meal
Main course only

7.30 pm – Notices and review

- *'Please bring your manuals for each session – there are spare ones to borrow for any who have forgotten theirs. Please use the blank paper for writing on and then transfer anything you write into your own manual'*

- *'Tell your fiancé(e) what you realised about marriage on Session 1. Look back in your manual to be reminded of what was covered'*

DVD: Play the DVD. Session 2 lasts for 54 minutes, but in addition, you will need to allow 40 minutes for the exercises:

- The benefits of marriage (at 12'17") – allow 5 minutes
- The marriage vows (at 18'06") – allow 10 minutes
- Planning time together (at 31'45") – allow 15 minutes (during which drinks and dessert are served)
- Parents and in-laws (at 42'58") – allow 10 minutes

This means the whole session takes **1 hour 34 minutes**.

Live talks

7.40 pm   **Talk** – *Why marriage?*

7.55 pm   **Exercise** – The benefits of marriage

8 pm   **Talk** – *The marriage covenant*

8.10 pm   **Exercise** – The marriage vows

8.20 pm   **Talk** – *Spending time together*

8.45 pm   **Exercise** – Planning time together
(during which coffee, tea and dessert are served)

9 pm   **Talk** – *The change of loyalties*

9.15 pm   **Exercise** – Parents and in-laws

9.25 pm   **Testimony** – By a married couple who talk about 'marriage time' and developing their relationship with their parents and in-laws (or show testimony on DVD)

9.30 pm   **Conclusion**

- Allowing time apart – this introduces the homework for Session 2

- Read Philippians 2:1–7 (or show reading on the *Inserts* available online)

- End with a short prayer eg *'Lord, thank you for your commitment to us. Thank you that you came to serve us. Please help us to serve each other and to live out our commitment to one another throughout our marriage. Amen'*

Session 3 – Resolving Conflict

1. Overview

Conflict can either destroy a marriage or, if handled well, strengthen it. Couples consider how to handle anger, appreciate their differences, look for solutions together and practise forgiveness. Organising finances, a primary cause of conflict in marriage, is also addressed.

2. Resources

- *The Marriage Book* – Sections 4 and 5 and Appendix 3
- *The Marriage Preparation Course* script for Session 3 (available online for live talks)
- *The Marriage Preparation Course Inserts* (available online for live talks)
- *The Marriage Preparation Course* DVD, Session 3

3. Checklist

- As for Session 1
- Spare guest manuals

4. Timetable

From 6.45 pm

Welcome guests with a drink

7 pm – Meal

Main course only

7.30 pm – Review

- Do a short reminder of the main topics covered on Sessions 1 and 2
- *'Ask your fiancé(e) what was most important for them from the last session'*

DVD: Play the DVD. Session 3 lasts for 55 minutes, but in addition, you will need to allow 40 minutes for the exercises:

- Rhinos and hedgehogs? (at 10'55") – allow 5 minutes
- Look at your differences (at 23'19") – allow 10 minutes
- Using the six steps (at 35'07") – allow 15 minutes (during which drinks and dessert are served)
- Discussing your finances (at 40'24") – allow 10 minutes

This means the whole session takes **1 hour 35 minutes.**

Live talks

7.40 pm **Talk** – *Expecting conflict and handling anger*

7.50 pm **Exercise** – Rhinos and hedgehogs

7.55 pm **Talk** – *Accepting our differences*

8.10 pm **Exercise** – Look at your differences

8.20 pm **Talk** – *Looking for solutions*

8.35 pm **Exercise** – Using the six steps
(during which coffee, tea and dessert are served)

8.50 pm **Talk** – *Dealing with finances*

9 pm **Exercise** – Discussing your finances

9.10 pm **Talk** – *Forgiving each other*

9.25 pm **Testimony** – By a married couple who talk about the effect of the differences between them on their marriage and what has been important for them in resolving conflict (or show testimony on DVD)

9.30 pm **Conclusion**

- Read 1 Corinthians 13:4–8
  (or show reading on the *Inserts* available online)

- End with a short prayer eg *'Thank you Lord that you are so patient and so kind towards us. Thank that you forgive us. Please fill us with your love. Help us to forgive each other and to keep no record of each other's wrongs. Amen'*

Session 4 – Keeping Love Alive

1. Overview

Love must be deliberately nurtured in a marriage. Couples do this through nurturing their friendship, discovering how the other feels loved and developing their sexual relationship.

2. Resources

- *The Marriage Book* – Section 3 and 7 and Appendix 2
- *The Marriage Preparation Course* script for Session 4 (available online for live talks)
- *The Marriage Preparation Course Inserts* (available online for live talks)
- *The Marriage Preparation Course* DVD, Session 4

3. Checklist

- As for Session 1
- Spare guest manuals

4. Timetable

From 6.45 pm

Welcome guests with a drink

7 pm – Meal

Main course only

7.30 pm – Review

- Do a short reminder of the main topics covered on Sessions 1–3
- *'Ask your fiancé(e) what was most important for them from the last session'*

DVD: Play the DVD. Session 4 lasts for 58 minutes, but in addition, you will need to allow 40 minutes for the exercises:

- Building friendship (at 9'50") – allow 10 minutes
- Discover your 'love languages' (at 20'34") – allow 10 minutes (during which drinks and dessert are served)
- Sex and commitment (at 34'38") – allow 10 minutes
- Talking about sex (at 52'05") – allow 10 minutes

This means the whole session takes 1 hour 38 minutes.

Live talks

7.40 pm **Talk** – *Developing our friendship*

7.50 pm **Exercise** – Building friendship

8 pm **Talk** – *Discovering each other's needs*

8.15 pm **Exercise** – Discover your 'love languages'

8.25 pm **Talk** – *Building our sexual relationship*

8.45 pm **Exercise** – Sex and commitment
(during which coffee, tea and dessert are served)

8.55 pm **Talk** – *How to build your sexual relationship*

9.15 pm **Exercise** – Talking about sex

9.25 pm **Testimony** – By a married couple who talk about their own experience of the topics covered (or show testimony on DVD)

9.30 pm **Conclusion**

- Read Song of Songs 8:6–7 and Psalm 85:10–13 (or show reading on the *Inserts* available online)

- End with a short prayer eg *'Thank you Lord for the wonderful gift of sexual intimacy. Please teach us how to use this gift to express and to receive love. And we pray that, in each marriage and future marriage represented here, love and faithfulness would meet together. Amen'*

Session 5 – Shared Goals and Values

1. Overview

While appreciating their differences, couples need to agree on their goals, core beliefs and values. They have the opportunity to discuss their priorities for the future, the roles they each expect to fulfil and the building of spiritual togetherness.

2. Resources

- *The Marriage Book* – Sections 10 and Appendix 4

- *The Marriage Preparation Course* script for Session 5 (available online for live talks)

- *The Marriage Preparation Course Inserts* (available online for live talks)

- *The Marriage Preparation Course* DVD, Session 5

3. Checklist

- As for Session 1
- Spare guest manuals
- The Marriage Preparation Course questionnaires (one per guest) – see Appendix 2 (also available to download from the Relationship Central website)
- Invitations to the next Marriage Preparation Course
- Invitations to The Marriage Course
- Invitations to Alpha

4. Timetable

From 6.45 pm

Welcome guests with a drink

7 pm – Meal

Main course only

7.30 pm – Notices

- Encourage guests to take invitations to the next Marriage Preparation Course to give to friends who are engaged

- Encourage them to take invitations to The Marriage Course to give away to friends who are already married. Explain that the content and format of The Marriage Course is similar to this course but it is designed for married couples and that more time is spent on some of the topics. Recommend they do The Marriage Course themselves two years or so into their marriage, or sooner if they feel the need to

- Explain that Alpha is for anyone who wants to explore the Christian faith. In this session we look at the difference that a joint faith can make to a marriage. Alpha is a good way of discussing spiritual issues together. Say there are invitations on the book table and they would be very welcome to come to the next Alpha on their own or together as a couple

- Ask them each to fill in The Marriage Preparation Course questionnaire. This serves two purposes. First, it is a good reminder for them of the topics we have covered on the course. It therefore acts as the 'review' of what they've covered so far. Secondly it is a great help to us in developing the course for other engaged couples. We ask them to answer as honestly as they can and we give them a few minutes at the end to make comments on this final session

DVD: Play the DVD. Session 5 lasts for 54 minutes, but in addition, you will need to allow 40 minutes for the exercises:

- Expressing appreciation (at 13'32") – allow 10 minutes
- Living out your values (at 29'14") – allow 15 minutes (during which drinks and dessert are served)
- Roles and responsibilities (at 40'55") – allow 10 minutes
- Spiritual togetherness (at 45'45") – allow 5 minutes

This means the whole session takes **1 hour 34 minutes.**

Live talks

7.45 pm **Talk** – *Matching our strides*

8 pm **Exercise** – Expressing appreciation

8.10 pm **Talk** – *Working out our values*

8.30 pm **Exercise** – Living out your values
(during which coffee, tea and dessert are served)

8.45 pm **Talk** – *Creating an equal partnership*

9 pm **Exercise** – Roles and responsibilities

9.10 pm **Talk** – *Building spiritual togetherness*

9.20 pm **Exercise** – Spiritual togetherness

9.25 pm **Testimony** – By a married couple who talk about
how they have worked out different roles in their own
marriage and the difference it makes to them to have a
common faith and/or to pray with and for each other (or
show testimony on the DVD)

9.30 pm **Conclusion**

- Read 1 John 4:7–8; 13–19
  (or show reading on the *Inserts* available online)

- End with a short prayer eg '*Lord, thank you that we
  can know and rely on the love that you have for us.
  Please bless every couple here in their love for each
  other. May their marriage be a source of great joy and
  encouragement to them and to many others. We ask
  that you guard and strengthen their relationship, and
  help them to build a marriage that lasts a lifetime. We
  ask this in Jesus' name. Amen*'

D. Couple Survey and notes for support couples

Couple Survey

The Couple Survey has been developed to work together with The Marriage Preparation Course and uses the same categories and topics as the course. It aims to affirm areas of strength in an engaged couple's relationship while also indicating issues that may need more discussion. There is no pass or fail and it is not a test of compatibility.

The Couple Survey is not an essential element of The Marriage Preparation Course and is not yet available in all the languages into which the course has been translated. However, we have found it to be extremely valuable in giving engaged couples an opportunity to meet up with a married 'support couple' to discuss issues that will help them in their future together.

We recommend that you run your first Marriage Preparation Courses without the Couple Survey and then, if you can, introduce it when you feel confident with the material.

We encourage engaged couples to complete the Couple Survey about a week before starting the course so that the issues we address have already been raised in their minds (and have led to discussions between them).

We describe in more detail how to incorporate the Couple Survey on the Leaders' section of the Relationship Central website.

The course may also be used effectively in conjunction with other questionnaires such as FOCCUS[2] or PREPARE.[3]

---

2 The FOCCUS questionnaire was developed by a team at FOCCUS Inc., 3214 N. 60th Street,Omaha, NE 68104-3495, USA, Tel: 402-877-882-5422. Website: www.foccusinc.com
3 The PREPARE questionnaire was created by Drs David Olson, John Druckman and David Fournier, LifeInnovations Inc., PO Box 190 Minneapolis, MN 55440-0190, USA. Website: www.prepare-enrich.com

Support couples

Support couples are married couples who act as hosts for each session of The Marriage Preparation Course. During the course or soon afterwards, the engaged couples meet their support couple on their own to discuss their Couple Survey results and other issues that may have arisen as a result of doing the course. This normally takes place in the support couple's home.

The support couple's aim is to encourage the engaged couples to express their thoughts and feelings openly and honestly to each other within the framework of a listening and encouraging environment. We match the support couples and engaged couples by where they live and, as far as possible, by age (so that the engaged couple is not older than the support couple).

Support couples will not have flawless marriages. They need to be willing to share their own experiences and the realities of marriage from a personal perspective. They are not counsellors. They come alongside the engaged couple to discuss issues in a non-judgmental and non-prescriptive manner. They know that if an issue comes up that is beyond their own knowledge and experience, they are able to refer the couple on for more specialised help.

The support couples are drawn mainly from The Marriage Course. During the notices at the start of the sixth session of The Marriage Course, we describe The Marriage Preparation Course and the role of the support couples. We ask couples who are interested to make contact with us and then describe in more detail what it involves. If we do not know them well ourselves, we ask for a reference from someone with pastoral oversight. If they have enough experience of marriage (at least two years) and are suitable, we invite them to an initial training evening where they watch the Support Couple Training (available through the Relationship Central website on the Leaders' login section.) There are accompanying training notes, which should be printed off for each person being trained.

The combination of The Marriage Course and this training is sufficient for them to start helping on the next Marriage Preparation Course. The following notes are an overview of what is involved.

1) Introduction to the Couple Survey

(See Appendix 5 for sample statements)

- The Couple Survey is completed online by the engaged couple and the results ('report') are sent back to the Course Administrator for onward transmission to the relevant support couple

- Couples review approximately 150 statements on their own and mark each with 'Agree', 'Disagree' or 'Not certain'. (As the survey is developed further we will add additional sections and statements)

- When they have completed the survey, the couple is free to discuss the questions with each other. (This accounts for 40 per cent of the benefit of doing the survey)

- Their answers are analysed and compared through a computer program to reveal the areas that require discussion, either because they have a different understanding to each other or because their answers are different to the 'preferred answer'

- Each engaged couple meets with a support couple after the course to discuss the results

- The aims of the Couple Survey are:

  – for the couple to explore all issues that require discussion

  – for the couple to be sure they are ready for marriage

  – for the couple to have a realistic view of what makes a strong marriage

- The survey is not a test of compatibility

2) Interpreting the results

(See Appendix 6 for sample report)

- The statements are grouped into eighteen sections, which reflect the topics covered on The Marriage Preparation Course

- Percentage of agreement 70 per cent and above generally represents areas of of strength in a relationship

- Percentage of agreement 50 per cent and below generally represents areas that that deserve attention

- Look for the lowest percentage agreement to see which sections will require most discussion

- Each section marks at least one statement as 'Critical' – these are regarded as basic to a healthy marriage

3) Facilitating discussion

The aim

- The role of the support couple:
    - IS NOT lecturing
    - IS NOT counselling
    - IS facilitating discussion
    - IS sharing personal experience when appropriate

- The main aim of the support couple is to facilitate conversation between the couple, helping them to listen to each other, to share thoughts and feelings and, if necessary, to work for solutions and compromises

- The main skill is listening and guiding their discussion

Your preparation

- Prepare carefully beforehand, deciding which sections of the survey to cover and choosing the statements in those sections to look at with the couple (one or two statements per section are usually sufficient)

- Decide which roles each of you best fulfils to facilitate discussion (ie one of you may be better at asking the initial questions, the other better at listening and picking up hidden assumptions)
- Pray together before the engaged couple arrives

The discussion

- Take time to get to know the couple first – perhaps by talking over a simple meal (lasting no more than an hour or so) or over dessert and coffee
- Allow one and a half to two hours to discuss the Couple Survey report
- Work out how you are going to sit (a three-seater sofa or two chairs angled toward each other so the engaged couple can address each other is ideal)
- If they are Christians, pray for the couple and for your time together before looking at the report
- You might like to give them a copy of the Couple Survey statements
- Ask them if doing the survey has already led to helpful conversations between them
- Look at the results graph in the report with the couple only if you feel this will be helpful for them (see Appendix 6 for sample report)
- Otherwise, look at the different sections in the 'Couple Survey follow-up form' to show them the different areas (see Appendix 7)
- Talk about those sections with high percentage agreements first in order to encourage them
- Move to one of the sections with low percentage agreements and look at a statement where one or both of them have put 'Not certain' or the non-preferred answer

- Say to one of them: *'Do you remember how you responded to statement X? Tell your fiance(é) why you put that answer.'* (Some areas of disagreement will no longer be relevant as they will already have discussed and resolved the issue)

- This may start a spontaneous conversation between them. Or you may need to ask the other one, *'What do you think?'* or, *'How does that make you feel?'*

- Supplementary questions are provided next to each statement where one or both of them have not agreed with the preferred answer

- If they ask for help or guidance, don't give them your answer too quickly. Ask them to state what they think the problem/issue really is for them, so they own the question for themselves. Then be willing to share from your own experience and suggest strategies you have found helpful in your own marriage

- Do not feel you have to cover every statement over which they disagree. Choosing one or two key items for discussion in a given section often covers the whole area

- Leave enough time to ask if there is anything else that they would like to discuss

- Invite them back for another session if you feel that is necessary

- Ask if they would like you to pray for them before they go. Couples who are not involved in a church often appreciate this offer, but should feel completely free to decline

- Have an Alpha invitation to give them if they express an interest in exploring spiritual issues further

- Give them the 'Couple Survey follow-up form' (Appendix 7) to take away with them, indicating further statements or topics for them to discuss on their own. This form is the last page of the Couple Survey report

- If this is the last (or only) meeting with the couple, destroy your copy of their report

4) Dealing with sensitive issues

- If you feel out of your depth with any issues that come up in your discussions, do not be afraid to tell the couple that this area is beyond your own experience. Ask them if they would like you to refer them for more specialised help. If so ask the course leader(s) how to proceed

- Cohabitation – this is addressed in Session 4 of The Marriage Preparation Course. Respond to their questions and concerns rather than initiating your own opinions

- Homosexuality – if this is revealed by one or other of them through the survey as an area they are concerned about, help them to express this to each other. If they want more guidance and support which is beyond your own abilities, ask the course leader(s) where to refer them for more specialised help

- High levels of disagreement – the issue is not whether you think they are wise to be getting married. Your time with them will draw out the areas of difference/disagreement and help them decide as they reflect on the important issues

- Addictions – marriage itself will not automatically lead to changes in behaviour. The couple needs to understand that they will not be able to change each other after marriage. Your discussion might help them to be realistic about the effect of any addictive behaviour on their relationship. Refer them for more specialised help if they request this

- Uncertainty about marriage – the course, the survey and your time with them will all help either to reinforce their doubts and fears or to lessen them. You may need them to help distinguish between a fear of commitment (marriage takes courage) and a fear that they are marrying the wrong person. Of course, the decision about whether or not to marry is theirs, not ours. See *Ready for Marriage?* with its seven tests of love (Appendix 1 of *The Marriage Book* and available as a separate resource)

- Pre-nuptial agreements – the most important issue is not what you think about such agreements, but whether the couple is in agreement with each other. If one of them is trying to persuade the other to sign, this can lead to resentment and an underlying lack of trust at the start of the marriage. Your role is to help them express their feelings to each other

5) Why couples should not keep the Couple Survey or report

- The report is not a permanent measure of the couple's relationship

- It is a snapshot at a moment in time – simple discussion can move them on quickly. Their scores will almost certainly have changed through doing the course

- It is a tool for discussion and not a weapon to be used against each other in the future

- It is designed for use with a support couple

- The couple can find out everything from each other anyway

- The Couple Survey follow-up form is more helpful for them to keep and is all that they need

- If the couple is insistent, please ask them to talk to the course leader(s)

Appendix 1
Suggested room set-up for
eighteen couples

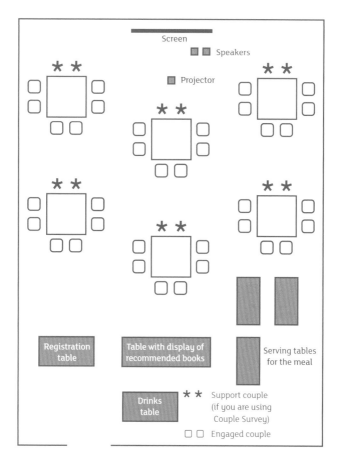

Screen

Speakers

Projector

Registration table

Table with display of recommended books

Serving tables for the meal

Drinks table

★ ★ Support couple (if you are using Couple Survey)

☐ ☐ Engaged couple

Appendix 2
the marriage preparation course questionnaire

This questionnaire is a great help to us in developing the course. Please answer as thoroughly as you can. Your answers will remain anonymous.

Name .... (optional)

How did you hear about The Marriage Preparation Course?

....

Are you a member of a church? ....

If so, which one? ....

In what ways, if any, has the course helped to prepare you for marriage?

....

....

....

What were the most important things you learnt on the course?

....

....

....

What did you enjoy most about the course? ....

....

What did you find most difficult? ....

....

Did you benefit from doing the Couple Survey? Yes / No

Please explain: ....

....

....

....

Did you benefit from going through the Couple Survey with your
support couple (if you have seen them)? Yes / No

Please explain: ....

....

....

....

....

Please indicate how helpful each section of the course was to you by circling a number, or leave blank if not applicable.

PLEASE CIRCLE 1 – 5 (1 = 'Not helpful' to 5 = 'Invaluable')

TOPIC

Session 1 **Communication**	*The value of marriage preparation*	1 2 3 4 5
	Learning to communicate effectively & exercise: Effective listening	1 2 3 4 5
	Session 1 Homework	1 2 3 4 5
Session 2 **Communication**	*Why marriage? & exercise: The benefits of marriage*	1 2 3 4 5
	The marriage covenant & exercise: The marriage vows	1 2 3 4 5
	Time together & exercise: Planning time together	1 2 3 4 5
	The change of loyalties & exercise: Parents and in-laws	1 2 3 4 5
	Session 2 Homework	1 2 3 4 5
Session 3 **Resolving conflict**	*Handling anger (rhinos and hedgehogs)*	1 2 3 4 5
	Accepting our differences & exercise: Recognise your differences	1 2 3 4 5
	Looking for solutions & exercise: Practising the six steps	1 2 3 4 5
	Organising finances & exercise: Discussing your finances	1 2 3 4 5
	Session 3 Homework	1 2 3 4 5

TOPIC

Session 4 **Keeping love alive**	Developing friendship & exercise: Building friendship	1 2 3 4 5
	Discovering each other's needs & exercise on the five love languages	1 2 3 4 5
	Building physical togetherness & exercises: Sex and commitment and Talking about sex	1 2 3 4 5
	Session 4 Homework	1 2 3 4 5
Session 5 **Shared goals and values**	The purpose of marriage & exercise: Expressing appreciation	1 2 3 4 5
	Working out our values & exercise: Living out our values	1 2 3 4 5
	Creating an equal partnership & exercise: Roles and responsibilities	1 2 3 4 5
	Building spiritual togetherness (& praying together)	1 2 3 4 5
	Session 5 Homework	1 2 3 4 5

What other issues could be addressed on the course and how could we improve the course? ....

....

If you would like to be informed about future Marriage Enrichment courses, please provide your e-mail: ....

Any other comments: ....

Thank you so much for your feedback

This questionnaire can be downloaded from the leaders' section of the Relationship Central website

Appendix 4
Recommended books

Nicky and Sila Lee, *The Marriage Book* (Alpha International, 2000)

Gary Chapman, *The Five Love Languages* (Northfield Publishing, 1995)

Gary Chapman, *The Other Side of Love: Handling Anger in a Godly Way*, (Moody Press, 1999)

Dr Henry Cloud and Dr John Townsend, *Boundaries in Marriage* (Zondervan, 1999)

Willard F Harley, *His Needs, Her Needs* (Monarch Books, 2002)

J. John, *Look Before You Leap* (Authentic Publications, 2002)

Katherine and Richard Hill, *Rules of Engagement: How to Plan a Successful Wedding and How to Build a Marriage That Lasts* (Lion Hudson Plc, 2005)

Mike Mason, *Mystery of Marriage* (Triangle, 1997)

Rob Parsons, *Sixty Minute Marriage* (Hodder & Stoughton, 1997)

Rob Parsons, *Loving Against the Odds* (Hodder & Stoughton, 1997)

Clifford and Joyce Penner, *The Gift of Sex: A Guide to Sexual Fulfillment* (Nelson, 2003)

Douglas Rosenau, *A Celebration of Sex* (Nelson, 2002)

Stephen Arterburn and Fred Stoeker, *Every Man's Battle* (Waterbrook Press, 2003)

Appendix 5
The Couple Survey
Sample statements

Circle Agree = A   Disagree = D   Not certain = N   for each statement

I am content about how we will share decision-making in our marriage	A	D	N
We have mutual friends who support us in our relationship	A	D	N
I worry that my partner might spend too much money	A	D	N
We talk openly about our attitudes towards money	A	D	N
My partner often becomes moody or critical when he/she is upset	A	D	N
My partner is good at apologising when he/she gets it wrong	A	D	N
I am confident that my parents/parents-in-law will support us in the way we bring up children	A	D	N
We take time to listen to each other's point of view	A	D	N
We are agreed about whether one of us will give up full-time work to look after our children	A	D	N
I expect my partner to change his/her behaviour once we are married	A	D	N

The couple fills in their answers without discussing the questions with each other and without seeing what the other has put. There are 150 questions. Their answers when analysed are grouped under different topics we look at on The Marriage Preparation Course and presented as a graph to show their levels of agreement within each category (see Appendix 7). A full explanation of the Couple Survey and the role of the support couples can be found on relationshipcentral.org/leaders

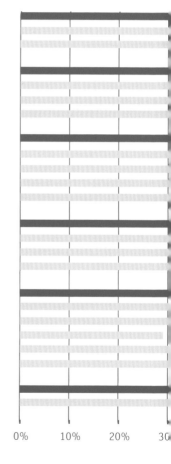

COMMUNICATION 67%
Effective talking 67%
Effective listening 67%

COMMITMENT 68%
Marriage as a covenant 67%
Planning time together and time apart 63%
Wider family 75%

RESOLVING CONFLICT 46%
Accepting difference 63%
Handling anger 44%
Dealing with finances 33%
Looking for solutions 44%

KEEPING LOVE ALIVE 85%
Building friendship 78%
Love languages 88%
Sexual relationship 90%

SHARED GOALS AND VALUES 67%
Matching our strides 75%
Family background 63%
Parenting 29%
Working out roles 75%
Spiritual togetherness 88%

READY FOR MARRIAGE 80%
Ready for Marriage 80%

0%   10%   20%   30

0%   50%   60%   70%   80%   90%   100%

Appendix 7
Couple Survey
Follow-up form

Engaged couples can make notes here so that they can continue to discuss issues brought up by the Couple Survey and read the relevant part(s) of The Marriage Book

SECTION	TOPICS COVERED
COMMUNICATION	Effective listening
	Effective talking
COMMITMENT	Marriage as a covenant
	Time together and time apart
	Wider family
RESOLVING CONFLICT	Accepting differences
	Handling anger
	Dealing with finances
	Looking for solutions
KEEPING LOVE ALIVE	Building friendship
	Love languages
	Sexual relationship
SHARED GOALS AND VALUES	Matching our strides
	Family background
	Parenting
	Working out roles
	Spiritual togetherness

THE MARRIAGE BOOK REFERENCE	COUPLE SURVEY STATEMENTS TO DISCUSS FURTHER
Chapter 3	
Chapter 4	
Chapter 1 & 20 & Appendix 1	
Chapter 2	
Chapter 13 & 14	
Chapter 8	
Chapter 11 & 12	
Chapter 8 & Appendix 3	
Chapter 9	
Chapter 2	
Chapter 5, 6 & 7	
Chapter 16–19 & Appendix 2	
Chapter 1, 8 & 20	
Chapter 13–15	
(See *The Parenting Book*)	
Chapter 8	
Chapter 10 & Appendix 4	

Appendix 8
Resources

How to order resources

Visit **alphashop.org** and **alphaprintshop.org** or ring the Alpha Publications Hotline on 0845 758 1278

For more information about The Marriage Preparation Course, The Marriage Course and other Relationship Central resources, contact us at relationshipcentral@alpha.org or ring us on 0845 644 7533 or visit our website **relationshipcentral.org**

The Marriage Book

The Marriage Course and The Marriage Preparation Course are based on *The Marriage Book* written by Nicky and Sila Lee. It is full of practical advice and is designed for engaged, married and cohabiting couples.
Book / Code 978 1 905887 39 2 / £8.99

The Marriage Preparation Course resources

The Marriage Preparation Course Starter Pack

Everything you need to get a course started for five couples:

1 x *Course* DVD
2 x *Leaders' and Support Couples' Guides*
10 x *Guest Manuals*
Pack / Code 5060059401963 / £55

Course DVD

Nicky and Sila Lee present the five sessions which make up The Marriage Preparation Course. The talks are interspersed with filmed clips of married couples talking about their own experiences of building a marriage, street interviews from around the UK and topical reports.
DVD (with subtitles) / Code 5060059400638 / £40

Guest Manual

One needed for each guest on the course. The manual highlights the key points from the talks and contains all of the exercises and 'homework' with plenty of room for making notes.
Booklet / Code 978 1 905887 47 7 / £2

Leaders' and Support Couples' Guide

For course leaders to use throughout the course. Follows the course content and contains useful information for leaders and support couples.
Booklet / Code 978 1 909309 04 3 / £2

Inserts DVD

(Also available on the Relationship Central website)

Contains all of the filmed clips of the 'sofa couples', reports, interviews and Bible readings from *The Marriage Preparation Course* DVDs. Those wishing to give live talks will find this useful for enhancing their presentations.
DVD / Code 5060059401062 / £7.99

Ready for Marriage?

How do we know that we are right for each other? What happens if we're not compatible? Is it normal to have doubts? In this short booklet, Nicky and Sila Lee address these and other questions asked by those who are contemplating marriage.
Booklet / Code 978 1 905887 51 4 / £1

Invitation postcards

A6 postcards to be given to potential guests.
A6 Postcards / Code 5060059401635 / £6.50 [Pack of 50]

You can buy and customise your postcards with your specific course details at **alphaprintshop.org** (Different prices apply)

Advertising posters

Available in A3 and A4, these posters are perfect for advertising your course in your church or local community.
A4 Poster / Code 5060059401659 / £0.75
A3 Poster / Code 5060059401642 / £1

You can buy and customise your posters with your specific course details at **alphaprintshop.org** (Different prices apply)

Introduction for Leaders (to The Marriage Preparation Course and The Marriage Course)

This short booklet introduces The Marriage Preparation Course and The Marriage Course to those who may be interested in running one or both of these courses. It outlines the formula required to run the courses successfully, summarises the topics that are covered and includes testimonies from people who have already led or completed the course themselves. The *Introduction for Leaders* also offers some top tips on how to start running effective courses.
Booklet / Code 978 1 905887 21 7 / £1.50

The Marriage Course resources

The Marriage Course Starter Pack

Everything you need to get a course started for five couples:
1 x *Course DVD* (includes 1 free *Leaders' Guide*)
1 x *Leaders' Guide*
10 x *Guest Manuals*
1 x *Leaders' Toolkit* (DVDs with CD-ROM)
1 x *The Marriage Book*
Pack / Code 5060059401970 / £100

The Marriage Course DVD (includes a copy of the *Leaders' Guide*)

Nicky and Sila Lee present the seven sessions make up The Marriage Course. Their talks are interspersed with filmed clips from couples who have been on the course, as well as street interviews from around the world. The DVD set also includes the talk for 'The Marriage Course Party', which introduces new couples to the course. In addition there is an optional session called 'Coping with times of separation', which is designed mainly for couples in the armed forces but is relevant for any couple who spends long periods of time apart. Filmed in 2008.
DVD (with subtitles) / Code 5060059401475 / £50

Leaders' Guide

For course leaders to use throughout the course. Follows the course content and contains useful information for leaders. (One copy of this comes included with *The Marriage Course* DVDs.)
Booklet / Code 978 1 905887 46 0 / £1.50

Guest Manual

One needed for each guest on the course. The manual highlights the key points from the talks and contains all of the exercises and 'homework' with plenty of room for making notes.
Booklet / Code 978 1 905887 20 0 / £2

The Marriage Course Leaders' Toolkit

Everything a leader needs to plan and administrate a course. The DVDs contain a filmed training session on how to run the course, promotional films for potential guests and leaders, and the filmed clips of 'sofa couples' and street interviews for experienced leaders wanting to give live talks. The CD-Rom contains training notes, helpful information and documents for course administrators, and the talk transcripts and presentation slides for live talks.
DVD and CD-Rom / Code 5060059401482 / £35.99

Promotional DVD

Perfect for showing to potential guests and leaders of the course. DVD includes:
- Guest advert – promotional film to attract guests [2 mins]
- Introductory film – describes how and why the course works, for potential leaders [13 mins]
- The Marriage Course Party talk – an introduction to the course for potential guests [38 mins]
DVD/ Code 5060059401444 / £3.50

Introductory Guide for Guests

Introduces potential guests to The Marriage Course. This booklet explains what the course involves and contains testimonies from couples who have been on the course.
Booklet / Code 978 1 905887 41 5 / £0.50

Invitation postcards

To be given to potential guests. These A6 postcard invitations have been left blank on one side, allowing you to add the details of your course using a mailing label or sticker. We recommend distributing these with the *Introductory Guide for Guests.*

Postcard / Code 5060059401536 / £6.50 [Pack of 50]

You can also customise your postcards with your specific course details by going to **alphaprintshop.org** (Different prices apply)

Party invitations

Postcard-size A6 invitations to invite guests to The Marriage Course Party.
Postcard / Code 5060059401499 / £3 [Pack of 20]

You can also customise your postcards with your specific course details by going to **alphaprintshop.org** (Different prices apply)

Advertising posters

Available in A3 and A4, these posters are perfect for advertising your course in your church or local community. They include blank space for you to fill in or overprint your own course details.
A4 Poster / Code 5060059401987 / £0.75
A3 Poster / Code 5060059401994 / £1

You can also customise your postcards with your specific course details by going to **alphaprintshop.org** (Different prices apply)

Introduction for Leaders (to The Marriage Preparation Course and The Marriage Course)

This short booklet introduces The Marriage Preparation Course and The Marriage Course to those who may be interested in running one or both of these courses. It outlines the formula required to run the courses successfully, summarises the topics that are covered and includes testimonies from people who have already led or completed the course themselves. The *Introduction for Leaders* also offers some top tips on how to start running an effective course.
Booklet / Code 978 1 905887 21 7 / £1.50

relationshipcentral.org